THESE SPARKS BELONG TO:

SPARK ADVENTURE

A JOURNAL FOR TRAILBLAZERS AND WANDERERS

CHRONICLE BOOKS

SAN FRANCISCO

ISBN 978-1-7972-2216-5

Manufactured in China.

MIX
Paper | Supporting
responsible forestry
FSC™ C008047

Illustrations by Kayla Ferriera.

10 9 8 7 6 5 4 3 2 1

Chronicle Books LLC
680 Second Street
San Francisco, California 94107
www.chroniclebooks.com

LET
ADVENTURE
LEAD THE WAY.

Set forth on your next life chapter.
Just flip to any page and follow the nearest
prompt to explore, wander, broaden your
horizons, and make new discoveries—
whether you're traveling or embarking on
an inner journey. Then capture it all in these
pages, in writing, sketches, doodles,
or any form that strikes you.

Blaze a new path! Your journey begins here.

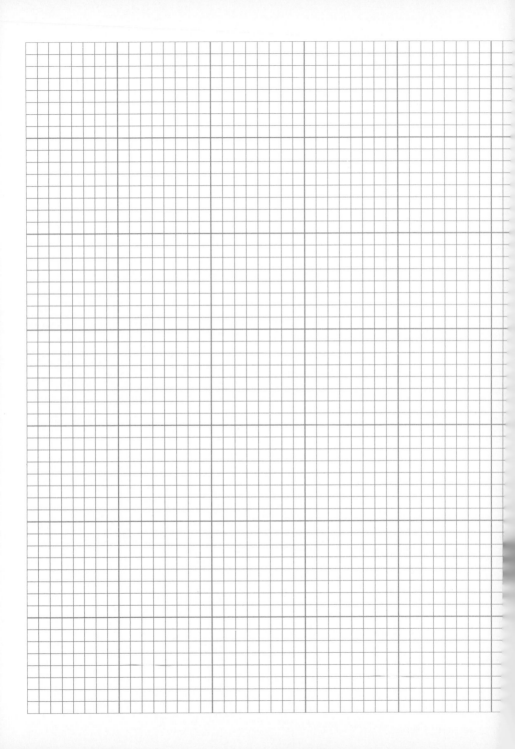

Try something you think you'll be no good at.

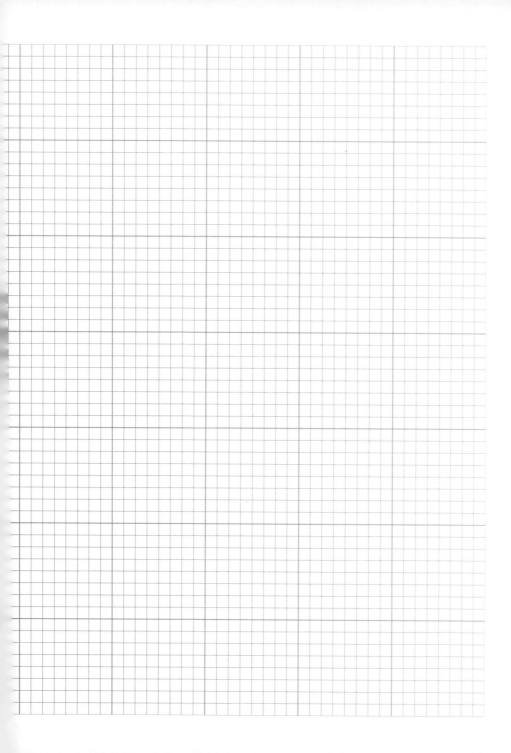

Make a bucket list and do the first thing on it.

Get your adrenaline pumping: Go climbing, skydive, or ride a coaster.

Ask a stranger for their advice or for directions.

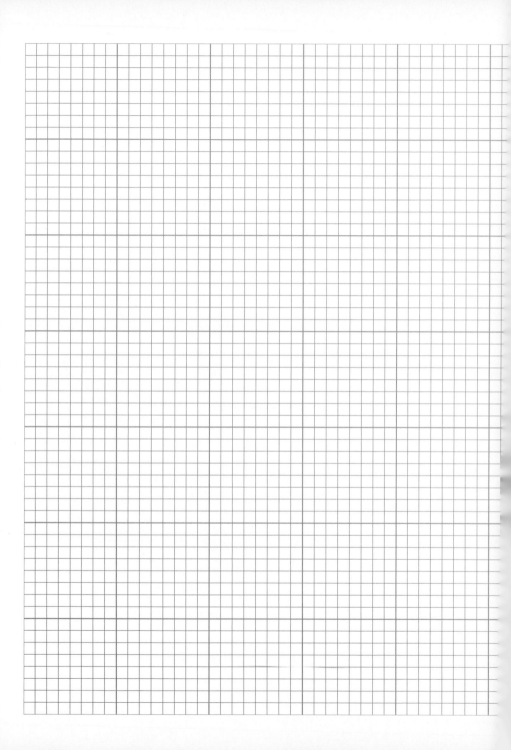

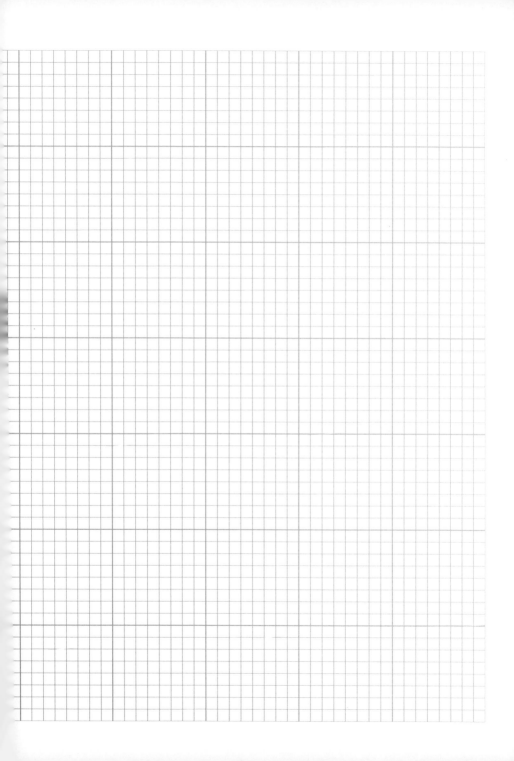

Look for the least populated area you can find.

PRACTICE SPONTANEITY

Try the slowest route.

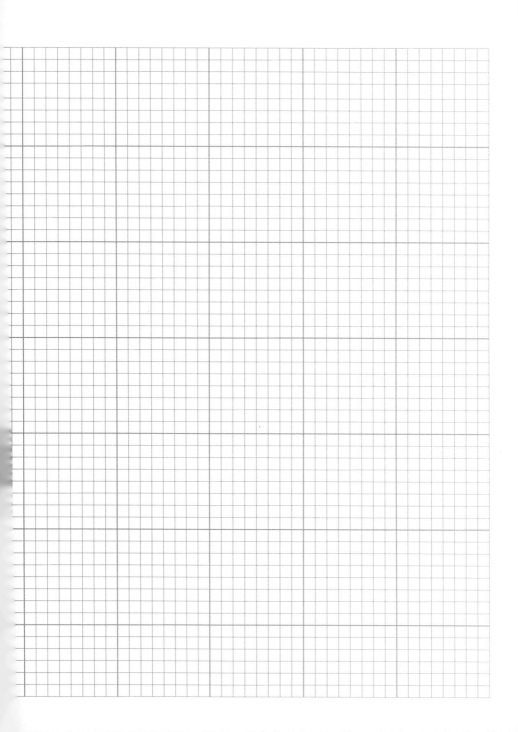

Shift your thinking: Visualize fear as fuel.

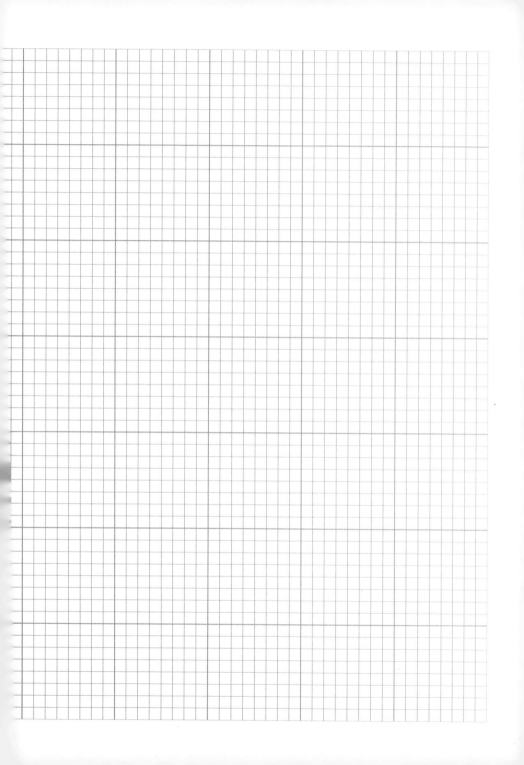

Do something that scares you.

Live dangerously: Go somewhere you're not supposed to be.

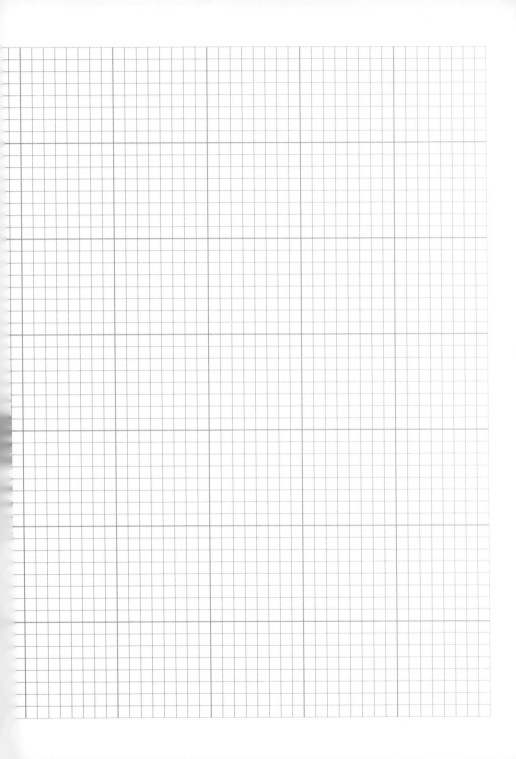

Write down your five signature strengths. How can you use one today?

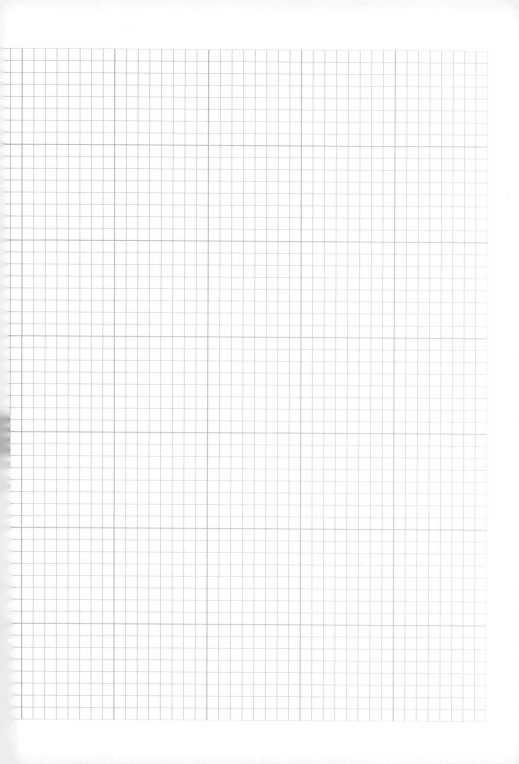

Get around for one day only by walking.

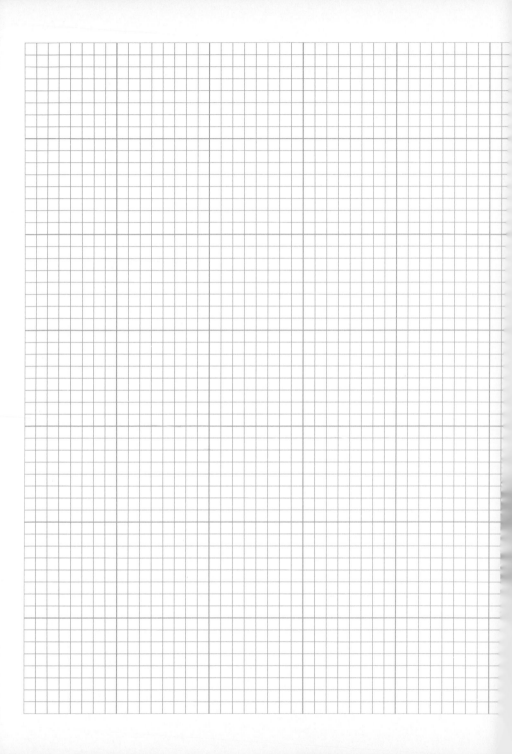

Get around for one day only by bicycling.

Embrace setbacks as part of the process.

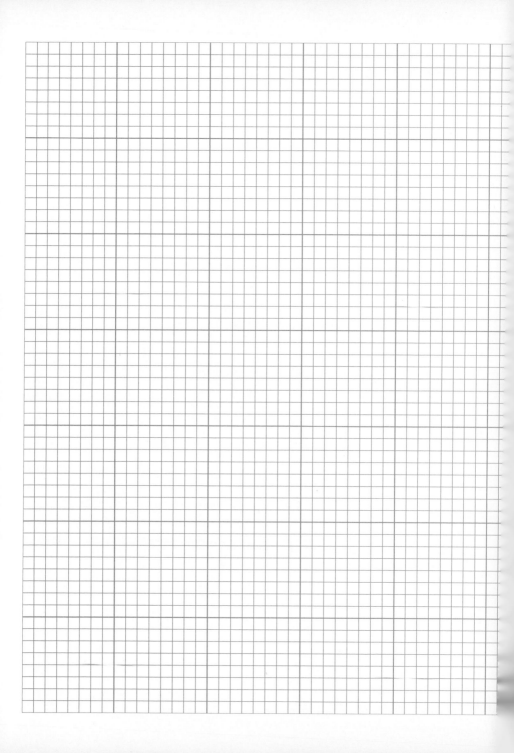

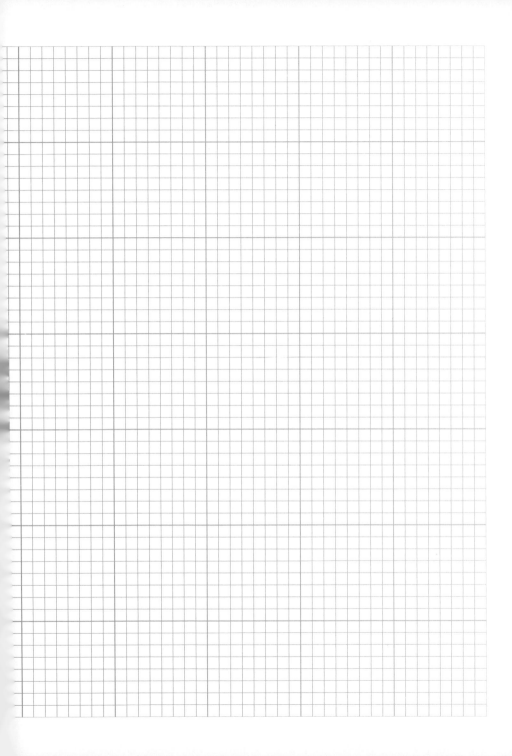

Be curious: Try asking every question that comes to mind.

Start a conversation with a stranger.

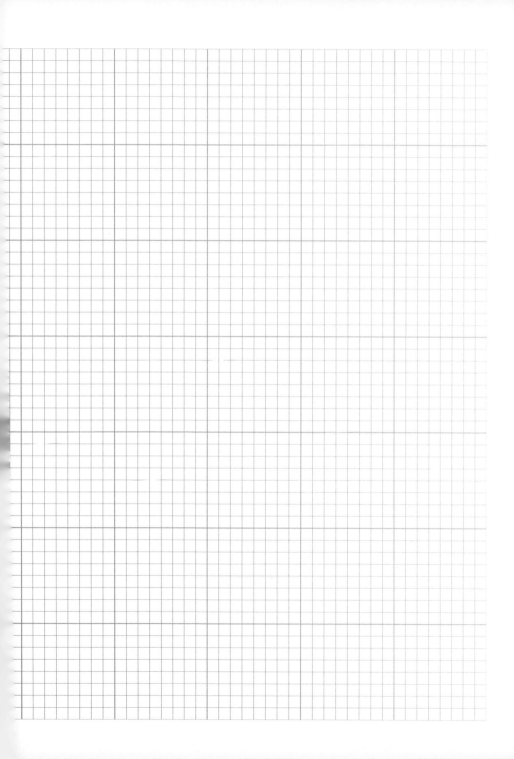

Wake up in time to see the sunrise.

Pick a spot at random on a map and go there.

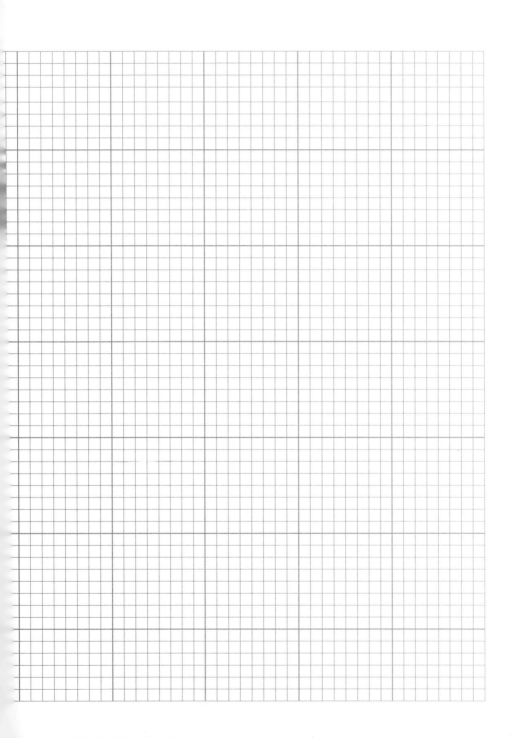

Take in the details and discover something you'd never noticed.

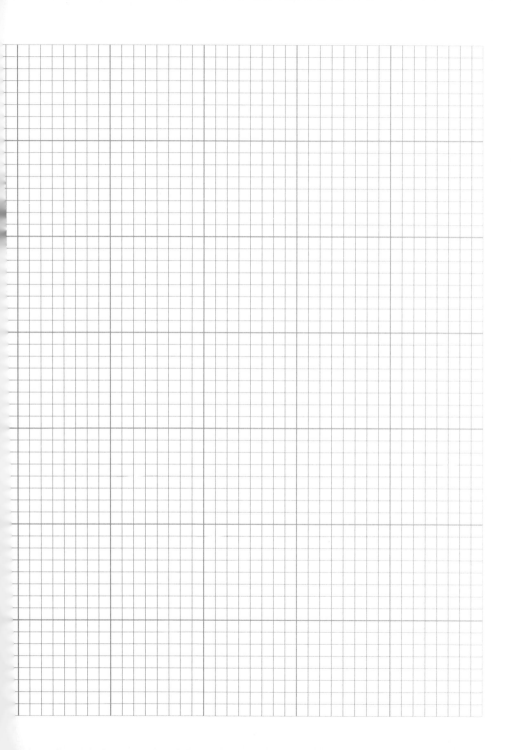

Say yes to something you'd normally decline.

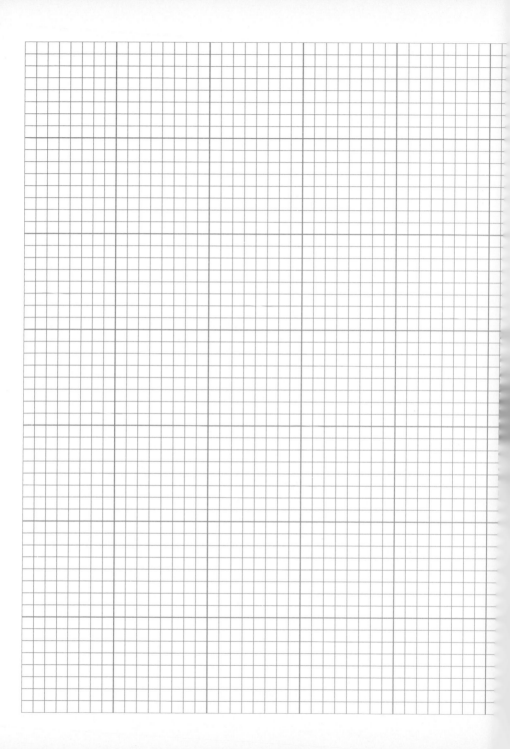

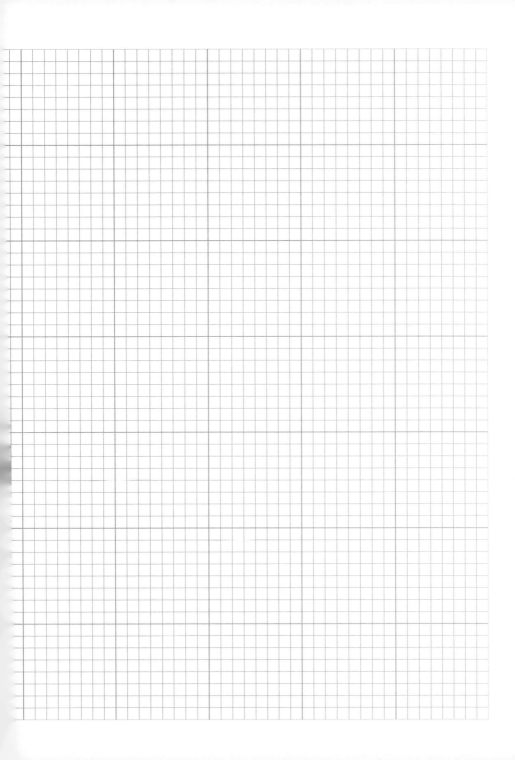

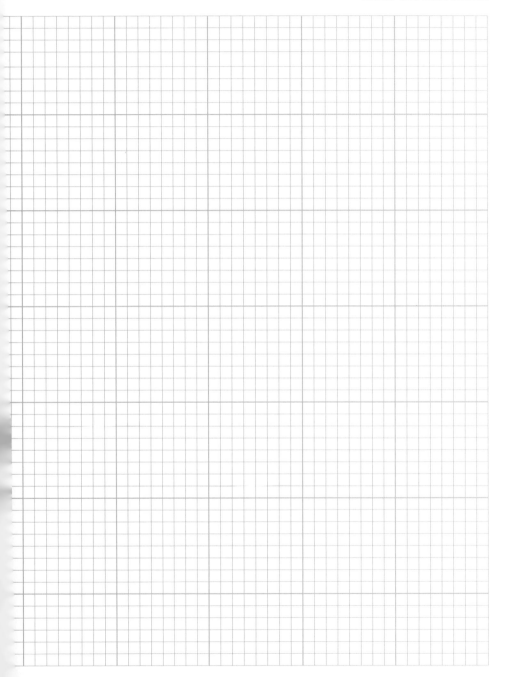

Break the rules.

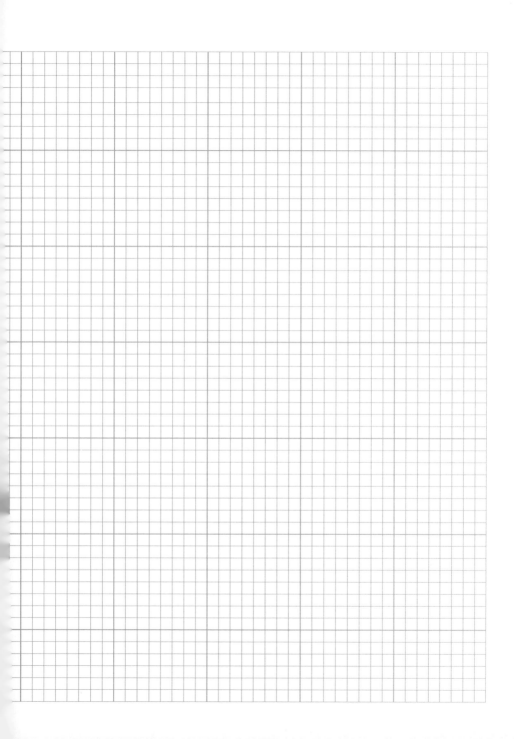

Take a risk.

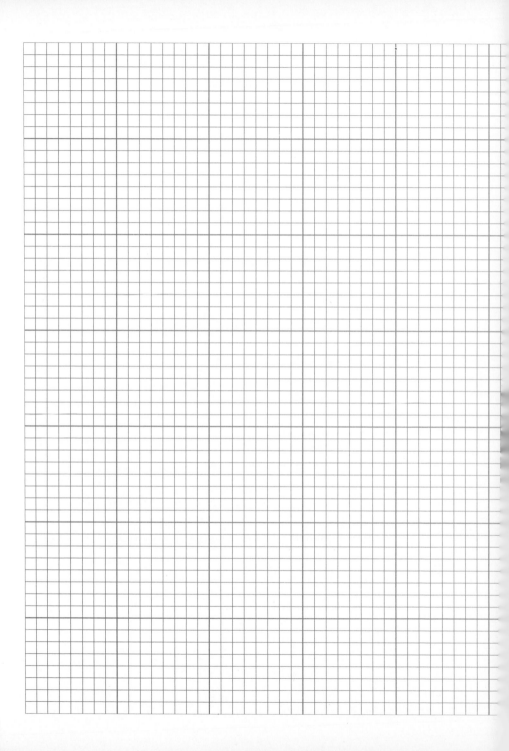

Offer help; be of service and see where it leads you.

EXPLORE WITHOUT A DESTINATION

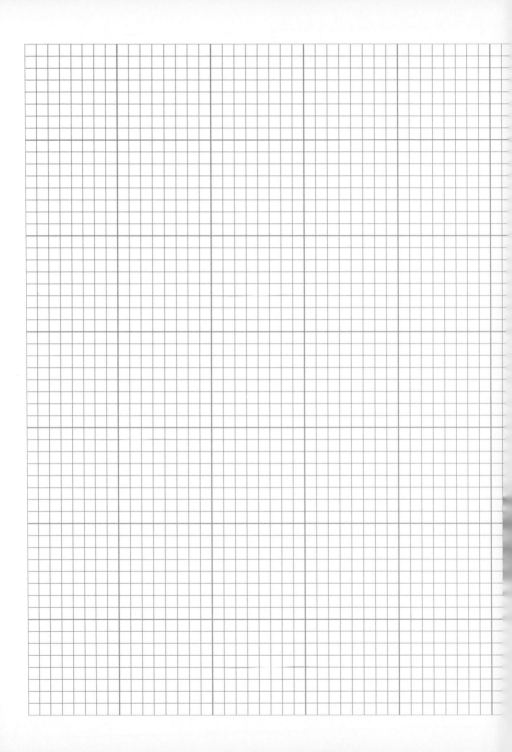

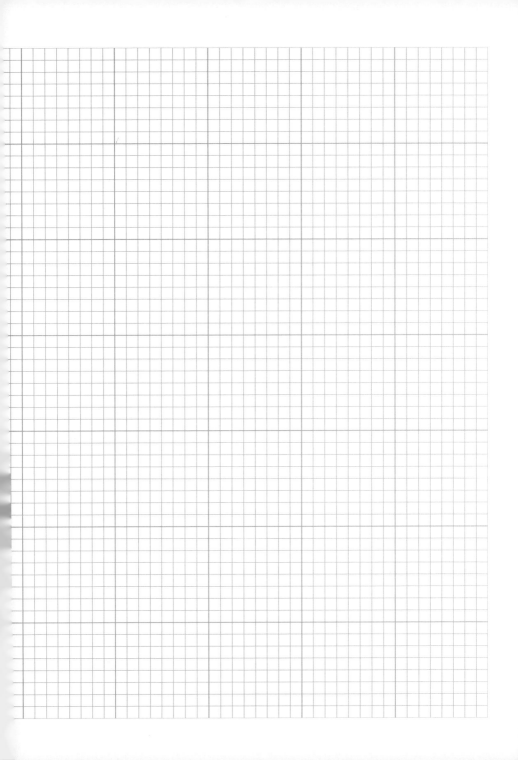

Practice a new habit.

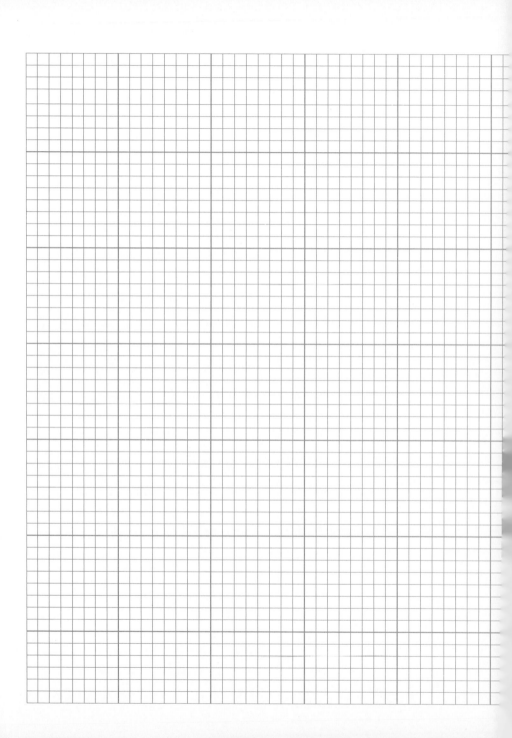

MAKE TIME FOR

DAYDREAMING

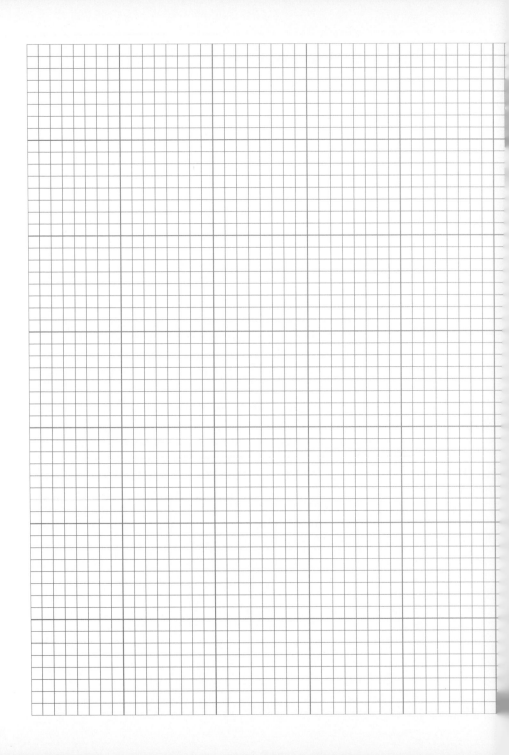

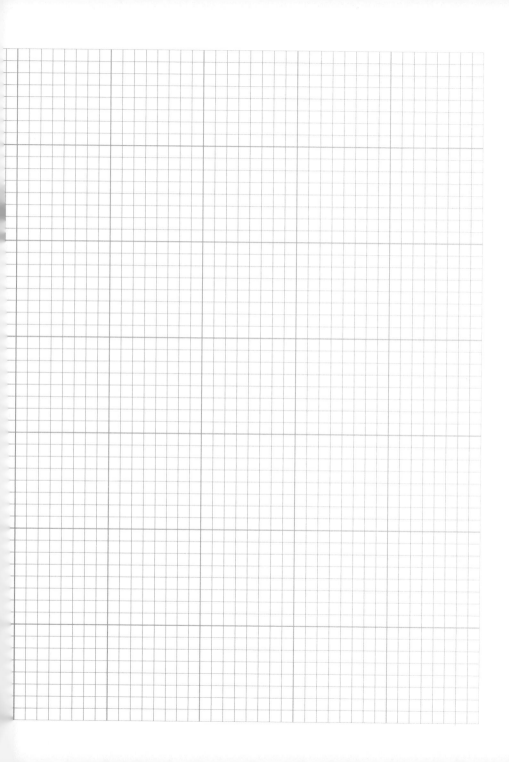

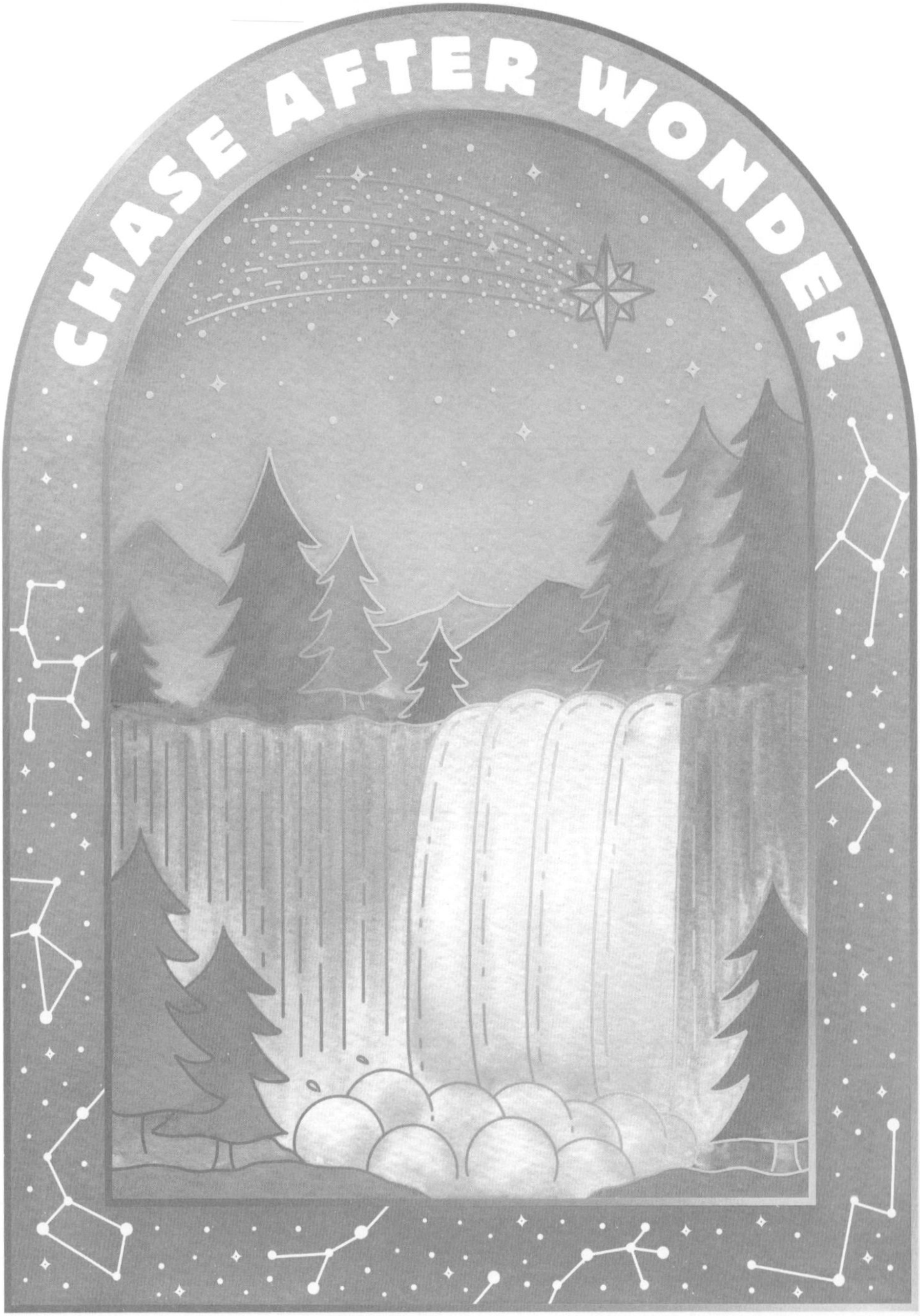
CHASE AFTER WONDER

Follow your intuition.